Our Global Community

Homes

Cassie Mayer

Heinemann LIBRARY

www.heinemann.co.uk/library
Visit our website to find out more information about Heinemann Library books.

To order:
☎ Phone 44 (0) 1865 888066
📄 Send a fax to 44 (0) 1865 314091
🖥 Visit the Heinemann Bookshop at www.heinemann.co.uk/library to browse our catalogue and order online.

First published in Great Britain by Heinemann Library, Halley Court, Jordan Hill, Oxford OX2 8EJ, part of Harcourt Education. Heinemann is a registered trademark of Harcourt Education Ltd.

Editorial: Diyan Leake
Design: Joanna Hinton-Malivoire
Picture research: Ruth Smith
Production: Duncan Gilbert

Origination: Chroma Graphics (Overseas) Pte. Ltd
Printed and bound in China by South China Printing Company Ltd

ISBN 978 0 431 19103 4 (hardback)
11 10 09 08 07
10 9 8 7 6 5 4 3 2 1

ISBN 978 0 431 19111 9 (paperback)
12 11 10 09 08
10 9 8 7 6 5 4 3 2 1

British Library Cataloguing in Publication Data
Mayer, Cassie
    Homes. - (Our global community)
    1. Dwellings - Juvenile literature 2. Architecture, Domestic - Juvenile literature
    I. Title
    643

Acknowledgements
The publishers would like to thank the following for permission to reproduce photographs: Alamy Images pp. **9** (blickwinkel), **13** (DY Riess MD), **15** (photoz.at), **16** (Neil McAllister), **17** (Anders Ryman), **20** (Petr Svarc), **23** (photoz.at); Corbis pp. **6** (Jan Butchofsky-Houser), **10** (Bo Zaunders), **11** (J. Scott Smith/ Beateworks), **14** (Jan Butchofsky-Houser), **18** (Jacques Langevin), **19** (Michael S. Yamashita), **21**, **23** (Jacques Langevin); Getty Images pp. **4** (Iconica), **5** (Image Bank), **7** (Stone), **8** (Iconica), **23** (Iconica); Lonely Planet Images p. **12** (Ariadne Van Zandbergen).

Cover photograph of homes in Narsarsuaq, Greenland reproduced with permission of Getty Images/Imagebank.

Every effort has been made to contact copyright holders of any material reproduced in this book. Any omissions will be rectified in subsequent printings if notice is given to the publishers.

Contents

Homes around the world

All around the world, people live in homes.

Homes can be big or small.

Types of homes

Some homes are close together.

Some homes are far from other homes.

Some homes are in hot places.

Some homes are in cold places.

Some homes are old.

Some homes are new.

Some homes are made of mud.

Some homes are made of stone.

Some homes are made of sticks.

stilt

Some homes are built on stilts.

Unusual homes

Some homes float on water.

Some homes are built on the tops
of trees.

Some homes can be moved.

Most homes stay in one place.

All around the world, homes
are different.

But all homes give shelter.

What are homes made of?

- The wood for homes comes from trees.

- The mud and stones for homes come from the ground.

- The bricks for homes are made of clay. Clay is mud. It is heated to make hard bricks.

- The concrete for homes is made of gravel, sand, and water.

Picture glossary

 **home** place where you live

 **shelter** a place to keep you safe and dry

 **stilts** poles that a house rests on.
Stilts keep homes above water.

Index

Notes for parents and teachers

Before reading

Talk about homes. Explain that all around the world people live in different homes but that homes are places where they are warm and safe. Talk about the different homes and ask the children to tell you what kind of home they live in, such as a flat, bungalow, or house.

After reading

Home song. To the tune of "Frere Jacques" sing a song about h omes: "Come to our home, come to our home / Here it is, here it is / We can play in our home, we can play in our home / All day long, all day long." Sing it again using different children's names: "We can sit in Rani's home", "We can dance in Ben's home".

Model home. Give the children a variety of boxes and materials and encourage them to make a model home. They might like to make one on stilts or with a thatched roof or even one that floats on water.

Book of homes. Ask the children to draw a picture of their home and help them to write simple sentences about it, such as "My home is by a road. My home has a green door." Put the children's work together into a simple book.